Echoes of America

A Journey through Verses

Dr Apurva Chawla

BookLeaf Publishing

India | USA | UK

Dedication

To my beloved mother,

The unwavering source of love, strength, and wisdom in my life, whose presence continues to guide and inspire me, even in her absence. This book, *Echoes of America: A Journey through Verses,* is more than just a collection of poems; it is a journey through the emotions, reflections, and whispers that you have embedded in my soul. Every word within these pages resonates with the lessons you imparted, the warmth of your love, and the resilience you instilled in me.

Your spirit, though no longer here in physical form, remains a constant presence in my heart. You taught me to see the beauty in the world, to find solace in nature, and to listen to the quiet echoes of the heart. This work is a humble attempt to capture the essence of those teachings, to honor the indelible mark you have left on my life.

Your legacy lives on in these words, and I
hope they serve as a tribute to the
extraordinary woman you were—my guide,
my inspiration, my mother.

You are forever in my thoughts, and your love
is forever etched in my heart.

Acknowledgement

As I bring this collection of poems, *Echoes of America: A Journey through Verses*, to life, I am deeply aware that this work would not have been possible without the love, support, and encouragement of many cherished individuals in my life.

First and foremost, I would like to express my profound gratitude to my late mother, Dr Bhushan Chawla, whose love, wisdom, and strength have been the guiding light of my life. Her presence is deeply felt in every word of this collection, and her memory continues to inspire me daily. This book is, in many ways, a tribute to the incredible woman she was.

To my father, (Retd.) Prof. R.S. Chawla, who has always believed in me and encouraged me to follow my passion for writing. Your unwavering support has given me the confidence to pursue my dreams, and for that, I am forever grateful.

I owe a special debt of gratitude to my husband, Subrata Purkayastha, my pillar of strength and support. Your constant encouragement and understanding have been invaluable throughout this journey. You have stood by me in every endeavor, and your belief in my work has been a source of immense comfort and motivation.

To my wonderful son, Anirudh Purkaystha, whose youthful spirit and curiosity continually remind me of the beauty and wonder in the world. You inspire me to see life with fresh eyes, and your love brings endless joy to my heart. I hope these poems reflect some of the lessons I've learned and wish to share with you.

To my sister, Anshulika Mahana, who has been a confidante, a friend, and a source of endless support. Your insights, love, and encouragement have meant the world to me, and I am deeply thankful for the bond we share.

Finally, I would like to extend my heartfelt thanks to all the readers who will journey through these poems. Your engagement with this work breathes life into it, and for that, I am deeply appreciative.

Thank you, all, for being part of this journey with me. This book is as much yours as it is mine.

With deepest gratitude,

Dr. Apurva Chawla

Preface

Echoes of America: A Journey through Verses is more than a mere collection of poems; it is an intimate journey into the realms of emotion, memory, and reflection. The poems within these pages are born from the depths of my soul, shaped by my experiences, my interactions with the American culture and people, and the silent conversations I've had with life's many facets.

Poetry, for me, has always been a medium through which I can express the inexpressible, capture fleeting moments, and give voice to the quiet musings of the heart. It is a space where the abstract becomes tangible, where the personal becomes universal. The poems in this collection span a wide range of themes, from the beauty and resilience of nature to the complexities of human relationships, from the echoes of history to the whispers of the soul.

This collection has been greatly inspired by the many roles I have embraced throughout my life: as an academician, a seeker of knowledge, and as a daughter, especially in light of the profound loss of my mother. Her presence, her wisdom, and her love have left an indelible mark on my life, and this book is, in many ways, a tribute to her memory. Her teachings resonate in the themes I explore, and her spirit breathes life into my words.

Each poem in *Echoes of America* is a reflection of the world as I see it—full of beauty, complexity, and often, contradiction. The natural world, with its endless cycles and rhythms, serves as a constant source of inspiration. It is in the rustling of leaves, the dance of raindrops, and the quiet majesty of the mountains that I find metaphors for the human condition.

As an Assistant Professor of English, I have spent years immersing myself in the study of literature and poetry, exploring the works of great poets who have come before me. This academic pursuit has not only deepened my understanding of the craft but has also fueled my passion for writing. However, the poems in this collection are not merely academic exercises; they are the result of personal exploration and an earnest attempt to capture the essence of my thoughts and feelings.

The influence of my time as a Fulbright Fellow at Fayetteville State University in North Carolina, USA, is the main context present in these poems. Teaching Hindi language and Indian culture to undergraduates in a foreign land was a transformative experience that broadened my horizons and enriched my understanding of cultural diversity. This experience has subtly woven itself into the fabric of my poetry, infusing it with a global perspective while remaining deeply rooted in my cultural heritage.

Beyond the classroom, I am a passionate practitioner of the art of scrapbooking, an activity that parallels my poetic endeavors.

Just as I carefully curate memories and moments into a scrapbook, so too do I weave words together to create poems that tell a story, evoke an emotion, or capture a fleeting thought. My interests in cooking and reading spiritual and literary works also find echoes in this collection, offering a glimpse into the multifaceted nature of my creativity and my continuous search for meaning.

Echoes of America is, therefore, a reflection of a life lived in pursuit of understanding, connection, and expression. It is my hope that these poems will resonate with you, the reader, and that you will find within these pages a reflection of your own experiences, thoughts, and feelings. Poetry has the unique ability to create connections across time and space, to bridge the gap between the personal and the universal, and to offer solace, insight, and inspiration.

As you journey through this collection, may you find moments of recognition, moments of wonder, and perhaps, moments of transformation. May the *Echoes of America* speak to you, as they have spoken to me, and may they linger with you long after you have turned the final page.

With gratitude and warmth,

Dr. Apurva Chawla

1. The Market Square

Fountain of life overflows with warmth,

The church behind greets everyone,

Those big black pots of green plants,

Like peacocks in the rainy season,

Dance with happiness.

The wrought iron chairs outside restaurants
and bars,

Like beetles, after the rain has stopped,

Sing the night song;

The sidewalk on either side of Hay Street

Is the place to be,

The Market Square in the center is its
majesty.

With a tall lemonade in my hands,

Mesmerized by the historical downtown,

I try to explore its soul.

With its multitude of history—

Beneath the cobblestones, whispers of the
past,

Echoes of footsteps long gone,

Yet the streets pulse with life,

Where time stands still,

and yet moves on.

The old clock tower watches with wisdom,

Its chimes a reminder of days gone by,

While the laughter of children fills the air,

Mingling with the stories,

The town's silent cry.

And as the sun sets behind the spires,

Casting long shadows on the brick,

I find myself lost in the beauty,

Of a place where the present

And the past gently mix.

2. Two worlds

In the shadow of old temples,

where the walls whisper tales of power,

the patriarch stands tall,

a figure carved in stone,

his words like iron chains,

binding daughters to their fate,

mothers to their silence,

sons to the burden of a name.

Here, tradition is a cage,

adorned with gold and reverence,

where the roles are set in stone,

and freedom is a dream,

stitched in the fabric of night,

only to be unraveled by dawn.

Women walk with their heads bowed,

their voices softened to a murmur,

carrying the weight of a thousand years,

as they weave their lives

around the desires of men,

around the myths of honor

that leave no room for flight.

But beyond the mountains,

where the sun rises unhindered,

lies a land of open skies,

a free utopian world,

where the winds carry no whispers

of what should be or must.

In this world, the chains are broken,

and every voice is a song,

echoing in the valleys of possibility.

Here, the earth does not hold you down,

but lifts you,

urging you to dance

to the rhythm of your own heart.

Men and women walk side by side,

not in the shadow of one,

but in the light of each other,

sharing the load of dreams,

planting seeds of tomorrow

in the fertile soil of now.

No names are burdens,

no duties are chains,

in this world of wide-open doors.

Here, freedom is not a distant star,

but the ground beneath your feet,

the air you breathe,

the very sky above.

Two worlds,

one of stone,

one of sky.

One that holds you still,

one that lets you fly.

And in the space between them,

we stand,

choosing the ground,

or choosing the wind.

3. If

If my hair were amber and skin light,

Sky would be dark blue, my life so bright.

If I could pray to Jesus, and be baptized,

Vineyards would be bottle green, my birth so prized.

If I could be single, and stay far alone,

My life would be mine, which no one could own.

If Hindi were not my mother tongue, and I knew German,

I could do whatever I want, having so much fun.

If I were not a Hindu, and belonged to the
world,

Earth would be Heaven, and Heaven, Earth.

If I could wear silk and lace every day,

Troubles would vanish, I'd be light as the ray.

If music were my language, and rhythm my
soul,

I'd dance through the world, my spirit made
whole.

If I could fly free like the birds in the air,

Boundless and fearless, with never a care.

If love were the answer, and hate never
known,

Peace would surround me, and I'd be
homegrown.

If dreams were my guide, and hope my light,

I'd walk through the shadows, fearless of
night.

If all could be simple, and truth set me free,

I'd live as I am, just perfectly me.

4. Journey to Home

While walking towards home in a Jolly mood,

I heard this sound which clapped with my foot;

Turning back I try to locate the tip tackle,

is it a little lovebird or a snake that rattled?

I think I heard it from behind the thorny bush,

oh! I hear it again and ask myself to hush;

Turning to my side I approach the sound familiar,

but from where did it come, is still unclear;

Is it a little squirrel cracking big nuts in victory,

Or some clever rabbits that have just run free?

I think I heard it from the hut made of clay,

oh! I hear it again and my ears are at play;

Turning towards the hut I walk with caution great,

I still can't find it, a feeling which I hate.

5. Life is a Playground

Life is a playground, vast and wide,

Where words and thoughts both turn and glide.

They dwell within, unseen, unheard,

In silence, they soar like a bird.

We speak and hear, yet oft we miss

The meaning hidden in a kiss.

I wished my words were clear and true,

But your sweet touch made things askew.

Communication, lost in air,

Turned into pauses, empty stare.

I hoped my voice would bridge the gap,

Yet silence caught me in its trap.

I thought of home, but felt a tug,

A grip so tight, like fate's own hug.

No space for me, or so it seemed,

Yet still I hoped, still I dreamed.

In pain, I cried, my heart undone,

Dilemmas choking one by one.

I wished my words were understood,

But silence stood where they once stood.

6. Where Shall I Go Now?

Lack of air suffocates, no breath to take,

Relationships bind me, with every ache.

Have I changed, or has time passed me by?

What once was sublime, now feels like a lie.

Years count as lessons, emotions as none,

Understanding's a joke, separation's begun.

This grief of parting will soon fade away,

Yet deep in my heart, it forever will stay.

The fire of love, though subdued, still will
burn,

That eternal passion now takes its last turn.

I thought it would last, but it flickers and
dies,

No more can I hold on to hollow goodbyes.

So I keep walking this journey of tears,

Where hope feels deceitful, deceived by my
fears.

My love lies in ashes, my dreams in the air,

The world is nowhere—no comfort lies there.

Where shall I go, when all paths are unclear?

Each road seems to vanish, with no one near.

The place once home, now feels hollow and
cold,

The warmth of belonging no longer takes
hold.

In a field of despair, where shadows do creep,

I bury my heart in the silence so deep.

The future seems dim, yet I wander alone,

For even in darkness, I search for my own.

I'll seek out new skies where the stars softly
glow,

Where I can be free from this weight and this
woe.

Though love may be lost, and dreams fade
away,

I'll find my own strength to rise with the day.

7. Waiting for Salvation

I see the desert stretch before me wide,

Orange skies meet orange sand on every side.

My eyes search for you in the fading light,

My heart aches to feel your presence in sight.

I reach for you, my hand stretched in despair,

Hoping you'll grasp it, still lingering there.

I stand like a statue, frozen in place,

The memory of you etched on my face.

The past replays beneath the golden hue,

The sands turn green as I dream of you.

Tears transform to pearls, wealth in disguise,

Yet my soul knows the truth behind these lies.

For richer I was in days now long gone,

When your voice was the only song.

When your touch was the world to me,

And in your eyes, my love was free.

Those youthful days that promised salvation,

Are now cursed by love's cruel frustration.

I stand where we parted, where we last met,

A crossroads of longing, haunted by regret.

From the depth of my heart, I still call to you,

These words are not the last I'll write, it's true.

Shall I hope you'll return, love once more
mine,

Or accept you've moved on, crossed another
line?

Hold my hand, or I'll fade without your
touch,

This separation brings a pain too much.

In this vast desert, endless and bare,

I need you to love me, to keep me there.

Yet the wind whispers a secret I cannot see,

Shall I wait for you, or set myself free?

The desert stretches, no end in sight—

Do I chase the past, or embrace the night?

8. From Spring to Winter

Spring spreads its wings in the wilderness
vast,

Winter is defeated, its hold overcast.

Oak trees release their yellow, dry leaves,

Making room for young green shoots that
weave.

Colourful bangles tinkle with cheer,

Bare skin shines bright as the sun draws near.

Silver anklets beat to rhythmic feet,

Spring's melody and music complete.

Long old love culminates in sweet wedlock,

The lovers' union, a love to unlock.

Mournful verses sing my elegy clear,

Marking the end of a life once so dear.

Destinations blur like a distant mirage,

As illusions turn real in life's collage.

The effigy of mankind is burnt each day,

Religion dons hypocrisy's sway.

Green landscapes fade into deep, rolling fog,

Winter's chill overpowers spring's warm log.

The frost-draped world now whispers cold,

Bare branches reach out, stark and bold.

Sunlight weakens, casting longer shade,

The once-lush earth is now slowly laid.

Winter's silence blankets the land,

A stark contrast to spring's vibrant band.

The hearth's glow contrasts the outside chill,

Warmth and comfort reside in the still.

In the heart of winter, old dreams lie,

Frosted memories beneath a grey sky.

Hope rests quietly in the depths of snow,

Awaiting the sun's gentle, thawing glow.

Yet with each season's shift, life renews,

Spring will emerge from winter's subdued
hues.

The cycle persists, the earth's grand design,

Where every end gives way to a new sign.

Though winter claims what spring once
brightened,

The dance of seasons is ever-enlightened.

9. Leave the Past Behind

Entangled in a web of emotions tight,

Immersed in seeds of dilemma's plight,

There's a world beyond the obvious view,

Behind the veil where dry tears strew.

Once my soul was green and pure,

In a garden I left, memories sure.

Thrown into darkness, I yearn for the light,

Longing for paths that once felt right.

Happiness dwells in a realm so mad,

Realisations bring pain, making me sad.

Wisdom's weight is heavy and profound,

Satiation lost where youth's dreams abound.

Crossing thresholds of tradition's old gate,

Entering age with wisdom's weight.

Breaking societal bounds, painful and steep,

Nourishing desires that dreams often keep.

Climbing ladders of ambition, high and true,

Living dreams in the mind, where reality is skewed.

Struggling against reason, seeking the self,

Acceptance of harsh truths, the only help.

Tracing back through history's faded lines,

Welcoming the future where hope intertwines.

In the struggle and acceptance, survival we find,

With each step forward, we leave the past behind.

10. Canvas

Today,

you are mine,

And I am yours,

We've become each other's canvas,

Filling it with colours,

Sipping wine.

If you wish

For our wings

To not be clipped,

Then come,

A little closer,

A little more,

Let's promise

To stay away from physical encounters.

Come,

Come closer,

A little closer still,

Until the storm of your breath

Creates a rustling in every leaf of mine,

And carries me away.

You are

Neither the body

Nor the soul,

You are an atmosphere for me, a vastness.

Before that depth and expanse

Shrink away,

Come, let's promise

To stay away from physical encounters.

Today, the fountain of love from your face

Races towards me, surrounding me,

And I find the ultimate joy

In sitting under the shade of the great tree.

Before that moisture

And shelter vanish,

Come, let's promise

To stay away from physical encounters.

11. Silent Depth

Many times, sitting in silence,

I wonder – I wonder,

Is it not possible that when

Everything outside is asleep –

Everything inside awakens?

That no waves arise in the mind,

No flow of thoughts – no surge of emotions,

No conflict of inner contradictions;

And the churning of dilemmas –

All comes to a halt,

Becomes like a still water source within,

A depth

That is mine,

Completely mine.

12. A Cry

Walking down the pavement of that desolate road,

I felt each heartbeat like an echo unfold.

A void consumed the depths of my soul,

The darkness around made my senses lose control.

In that strange silence, pleasure turned to bliss,

And the sweetness of pain I couldn't resist.

Lost in the emptiness, thoughts began to creep,

Reflecting on my past, on memories deep.

It was never about what I gained or lost,

But the question of whether I'd truly lived, at
any cost.

In the stillness of nature, my heart beat slow,

Choking on dilemmas only I could know.

I screamed into the void, my voice a plea,

A cry undefined, wild and free.

It was scary, raw, and unsatisfied,

Yet somehow contented in the helplessness
inside.

The wind carried my voice, but no one heard,

Only the trees, and the sky, and a passing
bird.

I walked further, the road stretching ahead,

With every step, old hopes felt dead.

The moon watched silently from above,

Witnessing a life devoid of love.

I asked myself if I could still feel,

If emotions were real, or just part of the deal.

The road gave no answers, only more doubt,

As I wandered endlessly, within and without.

The shadows deepened, but I kept my pace,

Chasing something I couldn't trace.

Maybe peace, or maybe a spark of light,

Something to end this eternal night.

But even in this darkness, I found a calm,

In the chaos of the unknown, a quiet balm.

For the void, though frightening, held a
strange allure,

A space where existence could feel pure.

Finally, in the distance, a faint glow appeared,

A hope, a whisper, a life re-engineered.

I didn't run, nor did I fear,

For I knew the journey had brought me here.

With every scream, every tear unspoken,

I pieced together a heart once broken.

Still undefined, still unsatisfied,

But somehow, I knew I'd survived.

13. Green Pastures

Where the grass was green and skies forever blue,

In the city where I once lived with you.

There lies my heart, beneath the ancient trees,

And there rests my body, swept by the breeze.

The cobblestone streets echo with our past,

It pains me to remember how time flew by so fast.

I am in love with your country's every hue,

From Paris's rivers to the misty skies of Peru.

But more than these, I'm in love with you,

Though my body is here, my mind's in
Kathmandu.

I see you in every skyline, every winding lane,

In every foreign city, I still whisper your
name.

I asked God to grant me just one final plea—

To let me die here, or bring you back to me.

Beneath Rome's arches or London's rainy
skies,

I search for your face, but it's gone in disguise.

Believe me when I say I've lost my mind,

For love has taken me, and left me blind.

Never knew love could give such unbearable
pain,

Like the silent streets of Berlin in the rain.

My only solace is the love I hold within,

Though I know we'll part, my heart won't give
in.

The decision to move, though hard to explain,

Was worth every tear, for that love still
remains.

In the shadows of New York's towering spires,

Or the deserts of Morocco, lit by campfire,

Your memory haunts me like the moon at
night,

A distant beacon, out of reach but in sight.

Yet even as I wander through this endless maze,

45

The love I carry for you will never fade or erase.

14. There is a rainbow in my heart

There is a rainbow in my heart,

That I see each day from the start.

It makes my heart sing in joyful play,

And keeps me cheerful, light, and gay.

The colours are many, like my desires,

They keep my soul awake, inspire.

They lift my emotions, help me stray,

From indifference, they keep me away.

The fragrances are many, sweet and fine,

Shifting with moods, they intertwine.

They sway my thoughts in gentle array,

And keep my patience strong each day.

Though sometimes from reality I may drift,

In these moments, I find my gift.

For the rainbow in my heart will stay,

To guide me through life's endless fray.

There is a sunrise in my soul

That greets me at the break of day,

It warms my heart with its gentle glow,

And guides me softly along the way.

The light is bright, so are my dreams,

They lift my hopes, they make me soar,

It fills my mind with endless streams,

Of joy and peace, forevermore.

There is a garden in my mind

With blooming flowers, fresh and sweet,

Their petals open, soft and kind,

A refuge from the world's defeat.

The blooms are varied, like my thoughts,

That twist and turn in gentle sway,

They make my heart serene and soft,

From life's harsh truth, I slip away.

There is a breeze within my chest,

That whispers secrets, light and true,

It calms my worries, gives me rest,

And paints my world in shades anew.

The winds are calm, so is my soul,

That bends but never breaks in a storm,

It makes my life feel whole and full,

With love and light, forever warm.

15. Rowan Park

When you knock at my door,

the winter sun glazes

on the crochet tablecloth.

It might have been imported from where I belong,

I think with the blush.

I keep asking, "We will go down the nature trail.

will we?"

You have Kalidas in one hand

A Cuban cigar in another.

I expected an answer.

I keep asking, "Can I buy

herbal lip balm there?"

you don't answer.

Just your cat points

to the door

and we walk.

At the gate,

far beyond the green landscape,

You show me —

a congregation of trees.

Under those leviathans

I see a gathering of

White Lilies.

16. Fayetteville

Wandering among strangers, yet never alone,

In Fayetteville's embrace, I found a home.

Those sprawling fields at Rowan Park's gate,

Whispering trees where I'd sit and contemplate.

The colours of fall, like memories, would change,

Each street crossing felt familiar, never strange.

At Fayetteville State, where dreams took flight,

The halls I walked in the soft morning light.

Professors spoke, and I learned to see,

A world of wisdom unfolding in front of me.

The library's quiet, the campus alive,

It was here my love for knowledge thrived.

At Cape Fear River, the boats would sail,

And under the sun, my skin turned pale.

I'd wander downtown, through Hay Street's charm,

Feeling the city's pulse, its gentle warm arm.

Luigi's Italian, and Rude Awakening's brew,

The taste of culture, both old and new.

The Southern hospitality, the music, the food,

It shaped my spirit, it shaped my mood.

The BBQ joints, where laughter would grow,

With every bite, a part of me would glow.

At Bubba's or Fowler's, I'd spend my nights,

Each meal a memory, rich with delights.

America, Fayetteville, you're part of me,

A treasure, a love, in my heart endlessly.

The language I adopted, the culture I wore,

In every breath, you're forever more.

Though I've crossed oceans, I won't disown,

This piece of America, my heart's second
home.

17. Maggie

Maggie, a tiny ball of fur,

Soft as a whisper, gentle as a purr.

Fifteen years ago, we shared our days,

In Fayetteville's quiet, our little ways.

During Christmas break, the world was still,

You'd curl up by the window, a soft winter
chill.

Your small paws would patter across the floor,

A little explorer, always craving more.

I held you close, your warmth in my lap,

We'd watch the snowfall, your tiny nap.

You were more than a friend's little cat,

In those moments, my heart was where you
sat.

Now, I look back at those fleeting times,

Memories like soft, nostalgic rhymes.

You must have grown, whiskers long and wise,

Yet I still see you through my younger eyes.

Do you remember, sweet Maggie dear,

Those quiet nights, without a care, near?

I wonder how you've changed and grown,

But to me, you'll always be that kitten I've
known.

In Fayetteville, with you by my side,

We shared a love that I still hold inside.

Though years have passed, and miles may
part,

You left pawprints forever on my heart.

18. Water

Through the drizzling rain,

I see his figure,

He is not here,

Somewhere very far,

In the mountains perhaps.

Rain often creates misunderstanding.

Values are drenched and wet.

Through the misty pain,

I see his figure,

He is not here,

Somewhere very far,

In the deserts perhaps.

Fog often creates misunderstanding.

Relationships are tainted and fake.

Through the inner pain,

I see his figure,

Somewhere very nearby,

In my soul perhaps.

Tears often clear misunderstanding.

Love instils life's instinct.

19. To Live or Die

Anguished soul craves identity,

Contented self screams in rebellion.

Sad mind hopes for enlightenment,

Satiated intellect shrieks in defence.

Lethargic body demands activity,

Energetic limbs move in turn.

Death drive strives to set in,

Life instinct yells in survival.

Mind commands kingly respect,

Heart fights to disobey.

Where shall I go now?

Where you go, I will go.

Your God is my God,

In you lies my life,

In you, death.

You are the Creator,

You are the Destroyer.

Utopia is in you,

With you, bliss.

Nowhere is in you,

With you, the end.

In the void of doubt,

I search for meaning's light.

The echoes of existence

Resound in the silent night.

Questions swirl in tempest,

Answers are shrouded deep.

In your embrace, I find solace,

In your shadow, I seek sleep.

The struggle between purpose,

And the pull of the unknown,

Finds its resolution

In the seeds we have sown.

Where shall I go now?

In your gaze, my path is clear.

In you, both life and death converge,

The answer lies, forever near.

20. Bird Alights

Whenever I see two birds flying,

Numberless questions come to my mind.

Wish I could see their language,

Wish I could hear their flight.

Is it too hard to fly in the air?

Does it involve a big social fight?

When one of them alighted alone,

I felt lonely and dethroned.

An outer force snatched my wings,

And that patch of distance still clings.

I could see it fly high and high,

The bird left alone took a deep sigh.

It too flew away in the other direction,

I was left pondering over its action.

Now, when I reflect upon its flight,

It adds to my experience, makes me wiser.

In its solitary flight, I find a mirror,

Reflecting my own struggles clearer.

The space it left, the void it spanned,

Echoes the distance I too withstand.

With each bird that soars up high,

I see a tale of freedom in the sky.

Their journey's end, a lesson profound,

In their silent grace, my thoughts are found.

21. Memories of America

Having Everything Bagel became our habit,

And Sushi, Pasta, Rajma Chawal, we could never quit.

Wine, Peach Bellini, German Beer, our favourites true,

And Pizza, Tapas, Fried Chicken, we could never rue.

Dunkin' Donuts, Waffle House, Subway on our way,

Pizza Hut, Sakura, Bombay Bistro, brightened every day.

Pierro's, The Barn, Mediterranean Grill, thrilling us with cheer,

Mi Casita, Little China, Golden Corral, held
us dear.

Dedouxe's, Olive Garden, Griffins, a sweet
delight,

Apple Cider, Muffins, Grapes and Hops, on
our favourite night.

Long Island Iced Tea, Chilled Beer, each sip a
cherished part,

These places and foods remain in our heart.

Years have passed, and the streets have
changed,

Our favourite haunts, now rearranged.

Yet in every new flavour, and every fresh
scene,

Echoes of old joys still softly gleam.

The bustle of new places cannot erase,

The warmth of memories we still embrace.

Though these spots may now be far from sight,

Their essence lingers, a guiding light.

In every new adventure, a touch of the past,

In the paths we walk, memories are cast.

The human experience moves with time's flow,

But the heart remembers where it used to go.

22. Ode to Nature

Unbreak my heart,

Amend me, bend me,

O Nature, talk to me,

Make my life music with your love.

Satiate my senses,

Your voice has a rhythm,

O Nature, make my life a rainbow with your love.

Sing to me sweet melodies,

Your blessings are motherly,

O Nature, make my life holy with your love.

Cradle me in your embrace,

Whisper through the trees,

O Nature, soothe my soul with your love.

Fill the sky with hues of dawn,

Paint my path with light,

O Nature, guide my journey with your love.

Heal me with your gentle breeze,

Let rivers cleanse my pain,

O Nature, restore my spirit with your love.

23. Conference Room

Grey curtains, brown chairs,

People huddled around, their anonymous
faces.

Bodily presence, absence of minds,

Do their roots have any traces?

Reflecting upon the tainted values,

I often get the same nightmare,

That unknown fear of night

Often shakes me unaware.

Am I a part of it?

Should I live in pretense or quit?

Wisdom has not yet dawned,

Might surrender in years or beyond.

Relationships demand stamps of worldliness,

Do they realize love is in a mess?

I search for truth beneath the veil,

Of hollow words and cold detail.

Is there more than what they show,

Or is this all we truly know?

The mind drifts in endless chase,

While hearts beat in a silent race.

Voices speak but no one hears,

Lost in the rhythm of daily fears.

Does meaning hide in shadows dim,

Or is existence just a whim?

The weight of life, a heavy stone,

In crowded rooms, we stand alone.

Perhaps the light will find its way,

And love, once pure, will learn to stay.

Beyond the masks we wear each day,

A deeper truth, a brighter ray.

In surrender, we might find peace,

And let the endless striving cease.

24. Snow

The crackling of frozen leaves below,

Impressions of tires on the snow,

A gentle tap on my roof above,

The heap of white at my door, like a glove.

Snow—it was a beautiful morning gift,

Snow—it set my world adrift.

Two days of warmth with hot coffee in hand,

Watching the white world, so pure and grand.

Just you and me in that quiet freeze,

Wrapped in the calm of nature's ease.

That lethargy I still cherish deep,

That quiet peace I'll always keep.

Silver clouds in the softest light,

Painted the sky a pale, muted white.

The world outside in a hushed repose,

While crimson embers in the fireplace
glowed.

The stillness wrapped us like a cloak,

As whispered winds through pine trees spoke.

Golden rays tried to pierce the snow,

But failed to warm the ground below.

The silence carried shades of blue,

As time stood still, just me and you.

The moments frozen, yet they bloomed,

In that winter haze, our hearts consumed.

The frost-kissed windows, a frosted hue,

The air so crisp, the sky so true.

In this world of white and grey,

Our laughter danced and found its way.

The colors of winter, soft and bold,

In memories of that snow, we hold

25. Nightmare

Last night was calm and silent still,

The lights would flicker, then grow chill.

At three, when leaves were sound asleep,

I heard the generator's growl so deep.

Anticipating disaster near,

I climbed the stairs, my heart in fear.

The house a maze, dark shadows spread,

With "Die Hard" and "The Grudge" in my head.

I ventured down with trembling feet,

The basement felt like doom complete.

Last night was calm, yet strange it seemed,

The trees no longer swayed nor gleamed.

Nature whispered, sign on sign,

Warning me not to resign.

I saw my future, bleak and clear,

Unfulfilled dreams were drawing near.

I prayed to God, to see His face,

Surrendered to His silent grace.

Dreams turned to air, ask the grass below,

It nodded, affirming what I'd come to know.

Was God unfair or was He right?

Ask the sky, the grey of night.

The watchman cut the power's hum,

The silence settled, cold and numb.

Yet still I stood, reluctant there,

The street below seemed unaware.

Indifferent, it watched me stand,

But faith rekindled in my hand.

At dawn I scrolled back to my room,

No sleep to claim, just yawning gloom.

The nightmare lingered, sharp and clear,

Revealing nature's power, near.

Was it a nightmare or a dream,

That left me calm, without a scream?

Was it fear or growing wise,

An awakening in disguise?

Then with closed eyes I felt the road,

A dry leaf fluttered from its load.

Was it dead, or was I blind?

Was I faithless, or was it kind?

With a mind confused, yet heart so light,

I saved the leaf from storm's harsh might.

Brought it in, now safe inside,

And saw its frailty with softened pride.

In the end, it was nature's grace,

To guide me through this silent space.

The storm may rage, the lights may fade,

But wisdom in the fear was laid.

From chaos, calmness rose so clear,

A deeper truth now drawing near.

I faced the night, but found my will,

And nature's hand, though soft, was still.

26. Two Months of Separation

Two months of separation, a scorching blaze,

Like the sun's cruel grip on June's longest
days.

These weeks have slipped, yet each felt slow,

Time moved, but my heart refused to let go.

Tomorrow, when I see your face once more,

Will I feel the pull, the same as before?

Will your presence intoxicate, like aged wine,

Make me lose myself in a love undefined?

This courage I've built, a fortress of stone,

Fighting the ache of being alone.

Survival in a desert, vast and wide,

Where hope is scarce and shadows hide.

But my strength is fading, my skin wears thin,

The resilience I cherished is caving in.

Why have you returned to my fragile heart's
door?

Is it to test me, or hurt me once more?

Are you here to see if I've managed to heal,

Or to reopen the wounds I tried not to feel?

Tomorrow, when your eyes meet mine again,

Will I break, or will I withstand the pain?

I've wandered through loneliness, a barren
place,

Each day haunted by the memory of your
face.

Yet I've learned to stand on this trembling
ground,

But now you're back—will I still be found?

Will you touch the scars I've hidden away,

Or stir the storm I've kept at bay?

I wonder, will your return bring peace,

Or reignite the fire, refusing release?

Do you come with love, or with regret,

Or simply to see what's left of me yet?

The strength I've built was fragile, frail,

But now your presence feels like a gale.

Tomorrow, when I look into your eyes,

Will I survive, or be shattered by lies?

Will I stand tall, unyielding and true,

Or crumble once more at the sight of you?

You've returned to my life, an enigma, a test,

But in this moment, I hope for the best.

Yet part of me trembles, uncertain and scared,

Of what we'll become, of what might be
spared.

Is this reunion a chance to heal,

To rewrite the story, to finally feel?

Or is it a cycle, painful and clear,

That drags me back to the days of fear?

Tomorrow, when I see your face so near,

Will I survive, or disappear?

Will I rise stronger, unshaken and free,

Or lose myself in what used to be?

Two months of waiting, of questioning why,

Of searching for answers beneath the sky.

But tomorrow holds the truth, unknown and vast,

When I see your face, will I outlast the past?

27. In Soul and Spirit, you are always near

Your voice, like petals of roses, so light,

Brushes my ear in the stillness of night.

Though thousands of miles keep us apart,

You're always near, deep in my heart.

Your touch, like dew's cool kiss at dawn,

Slips down my skin, even though you're gone.

Though oceans stretch between you and me,

In your memories, I drift so free.

Your divinity, like peace of mind,

Is woven within, a comfort I find.

Though your intellect soars beyond my reach,

You are my guru, with wisdom to teach.

Your presence, like a calming breeze,

Wraps around me, puts my mind at ease.

Though miles and time may intervene,

You dwell in my soul, serene and unseen.

Your love, like moonlight soft and pure,

Guides me through nights, steady and sure.

Though our bodies may be far away,

Your spirit within me will always stay.

Your laughter, like a distant song,

Lingers with me, keeps me strong.

Though life may scatter us far and wide,

You are the anchor on which I ride.

Your light, like stars in a velvet sky,

Illuminates the path where shadows lie.

Though separated by lands unknown,

In my heart, you have always grown.

So distance fades, it means nothing here,

In soul and spirit, you're always near.

Though worlds apart, our bond holds true,

Forever entwined, in all I do.

www.ingramcontent.com/pod-product-compliance
Lightning Source LLC
LaVergne TN
LVHW011031200726
843509LV00011B/1244